L

Also by Suzanne Matson

SEA LEVEL

DURABLE GOODS poems
— by —
SUZANNE MATSON

ALICE JAMES BOOKS
Cambridge, Massachusetts

ACKNOWLEDGMENTS

Grateful acknowledgment is made to the editors of the following
publications, in which some of these poems first appeared:
*Berkeley Poetry Review, Boston College Magazine, The Christian Science
Monitor, Dominion Review, Harvard Review, Indiana Review,
The Seattle Review, Shenandoah, Sojourner, Sou'wester.*
"The Regulars" and "Wifery" will appear in *For a Living:
Contemporary Work Poems*, U of Illinois P, 1994.

Library of Congress Cataloging-in-Publication Data

Matson, Suzanne, 1959-
Durable Goods / Suzanne Matson.
I. Title
PS3563.A8378D87 1993
811'.54—dc20   93-14958   CIP
ISBN 1-882295-00-5

Cover and text design by Charles Casey Martin.

The author would like to thank Boston College for a Faculty Fellowship
which supported a period of writing time to complete this collection.

Alice James Books gratefully acknowledges support from the National
Endowment for the Arts and from the Massachusetts Council on the
Arts and Humanities, a state agency whose funds are recommended by
the Governor and appropriated by the State Legislature.

Alice James Books are published by
the Alice James Poetry Cooperative, Inc.

ALICE JAMES BOOKS
33 Richdale Avenue
Cambridge, Massachusetts 02140

For Joe

CONTENTS

DURABLE GOODS

ONE

PLATIA TALO

This is where they stand
when they are making postcards; it's all
here: lighthouse, crumbling rampart from
the 14th century, sweep of sea with border of white
foam—there's more—three horizon lines of mountains
in relief so that they are overlaid tissues
of pure color, or more nearly, absence
of color—the blue-gray of certainty
without excess, without error or possibility
of error. Even more, a moon
coming back from nowhere, if new is nowhere,
radically slim in its recovery.
It's the very sidewalk which hardens
us into a *scene*, which keeps composing us
from the angle of our invisible kinship
with strangers, this instinct of mattering
to each other, however briefly.

GREEK

He tells me I'll never understand
if they don't want me to. This I fully
understand—as I struggle with the infant
conjugations in my head
beginning with *I am, I have.*
You comes next, *we* is third,
and for the time being I ignore *them*
and *all of you.* My world
is intimate, primitive, a small
circle that begins with me and only
gradually acquires an orbit of other
concerns. *I want, I love.*
Money and time follow.
But if he doesn't want me to understand
I won't—him flashing bills down
before I've even calculated my debt.
Reckoning comes sooner than I think:
You must, you can't
—and here my words run dry
as we both understand perfectly
that with or without them we can resist each other's
sentences, those lessons in not being yourself.
The next unit is all about abstraction,
an exercise in faith. Go ahead and teach me,
if you can, stranger,
about *will,*
the root of the future:
I will stay, you will
stay, we will stay, until I abandon
my search for the conditional with all its
contingencies, its endless dry multiplications,
its small dark threat.

NIGHT FISHING

His illegal light stuns the fish
into momentary
paralysis so that for a moment he exceeds
the natural limitations of pursuit. When they hang
there, small blind lanterns,
organized in a pattern he can know
nothing of, map of their own forgotten intentions,
when they wait for him so patiently,
dissolvingly, and he pierces them and floats them
on their ribbons of blood one at a time
into his sack, who can say
he was wrong? Or that his hunger
and mastery were not the new law? Whatever is
becomes the law. The fish observed that.

CAFE

The wind comes up, dice rattle, the cassette returns
for another loop. And she is cold from it,
just as it begins to be easy—
inevitable—to be planning which bus
she will take on which day, which direction,
into the gray mass of mountains which could stand
for stopping, leaning against the whole mass
of rock and in the clean unforgiveness
of the hard scrabble, stopping. Or along
the margin of rock and sea, slipping around
the whole circumference of the island, keeping
the notion of chase alive in the quick, lubricated
dart of her circling. In the planning she becomes
free, and cold, and her sight brightens and hardens
around the edges so that the boy beaching
his dolphin paddle boat is a chip of landscape,
the flat color of red trunks, blue grinning
dolphin, rough black pebbly scrape of their arrival.
In so much small tilt of her shoulder and the force
of her focus—now the man on the motor scooter, all
circles, all rings of motion—he feels the shift
of wind, and leans a little toward the sea,
the side of him she occupies. The long angles
of his legs uncross a little, his eyes might have swept
over her once, if she had seen, had she not been
making small, discrete
bodies in the surf, each of them
separate and resolute.

THE BEACH

The boy and the girl toss the white ball
in the blue sea,
the blue sea glistens,
the white ball—*pong* against fists—
glistens
as do the bodies of the children
wild as alphabet letters.
They each overthrow the ball
shouting with pleasure at the strength of their inaccuracies.

The young men
hit the ball
to each other
on the hard-packed
margin of sand
before the sea.
They work their
crisp volley faster
and faster until
they have some-
thing between them
as hard and pre-
cise as a thigh
muscle, as clear
as a perfect
understanding.

The women lie on the beach like
unshelled mollusks. They lie
on the beach and turn heavily
in the glaucous mirror of all the gazes
they have turned inward since

the ball left their hands for good and they held cupfuls
of themselves instead to be measured against the heaviness
of a world turned inner, swelling from their own and
the world's excess which everywhere began cutting fine red patterns
into the flesh.

CHANIA

The clean new car, roses on its hood
and roof, presses forward through
the crowd. Someone, the father, leans
on the horn. Spectators break apart
to line both sides of the church plaza.
When the bride emerges, it is everything
we could have hoped for—satin tufted
closely to the young body, the scalloped
train sweeping ruinously through the dust
behind her. Her thick black hair is
sculpted into what we understand to be
a mane. Her lips are red.
Somewhere inside a groom waits
in his own splendor, but this is the real
moment, the bride as prepared and icy
as a cake, taken on either side by a
parent who has done everything
that could be done. This is the moment
that the crowd is moved to applaud—
expense, sacrifice, bestowal.
Oh she glitters
whitely
          with just enough fire on her mouth
to promise a young man waiting in the dark
everything, everything for all their lives.

THE WRECK OF DAYS

1

This morning the sea shows evidence
of its sudden turn—red branching weeds
everywhere uprooted from their deep places
of belonging.

Cigarettes and plastics tossed lightly from fishing boats
wash up, as if the sea needed to be free of its debris
and be solution, pure.

Three men are on that sea somewhere
who left in a new boat
with some expensive equipment
that no one had quite tested.

They are two brothers and a partner, all of them
invested, all of them thinking to be married soon,
now that they have the costly means of making
a way in the world.

Now they are six days past their food.
Now the tiny plane of their fathers probes
the edges of the island, searching the rocks
for the gleaming signs of sons.

2

Everyday I swam to the smaller island *Lazareta*
making up part of the sea,
stroking against its
white caps and colored ribbons of thermal shift,
glassy swells with dead weeds, or the
fat sea of a hot still day, the medusas hanging
festively poisonous.

3

Now they are eight days past food,
past water, past bait, past petrol,
now the younger sister of the pair of brothers
has been rushed to the hospital

her heart murmuring
eight days, eight days.
The mother sits fixedly by the bedside
and her eyes will not leave the machines that sing
eight days from her daughter's heart.

The father leans against his car in the street
arms folded across his chest,
he keeps his back to the sea.
Around him has gathered a half-circle of men
from the cafe where, two weeks ago
the boys traded drinks
to the boat, to weather, to the future.
Each man holds his hands clasped behind his back
and faces the sea, a chorus of watchers,
chorus of no news but speculation,
calculation: how far you could swim, how long,
to where, why you might have to, why you might
not. Mother and daughter huddle in the green thrall
of the machine. It registers *eight days*, it registers
life.

The father has turned his back to sea.
He has no need to lift his eyes to the wash
of moonlit foam and rolling scraps
that the sea refuses to keep. The movements

of the sea are in his birthblood
and now he feels large enough to contain it all—
every reversal, every tide,
so deep is his knowledge, so accurate
his tracing of the floor.

The men from the cafe fall silent and keep faced
to the sea. When one leaves to go home
another comes to take his place in the circle
so swiftly that no harmony is broken,
no small beat of silence lost.
They face the sea because they watch, even
in darkness. They offer the full
front of themselves, they offer to hold
themselves in place as long as they must.
There is nothing they will hold back, and,
for the moment, nothing they can hand over.
They present themselves.

4

I hold it like blown glass—sand and fire and water
and my own delicate breath—seven days remaining
on the island, enough, it would seem, to complete
anything, heaven and earth,
every element in its place, all possibility
set in motion. Seven days I hold in my hand like—not creation,
not that godlike precipice—but lifetime,
a way of being until ending, a series of accidents
to avoid, a mystery of my own to conclude
in my body rinsed and massaged by the sea's
astringent solution

while boats founder in their own stories
while here the men gather in the cafe to argue
endings. Sons are vanished without a trace nine days.
They too had their instant of setting out,
holding voyage like a work undone,
holding disaster like a choice,
holding us hostage to the salvage
of their wreck of days, since beginning.

5

When the black Mercedes pulled up along the seafront
the cafe emptied into the night as if the men there
were water draining toward larger water.
So that by the time the high priest
in all his slow lean majesty, in his deeply black
and radiantly silver self stepped from the car,
leading with his crook, he had his congregation. Reader,
the name of the boat was *Archangel Michael*.
There was still time, in the seconds
hovering there beneath the Great Bear,
beneath all the animals toothed and ranging overhead,
for nothing to happen. There was time
before words. And like you searching
the page for the rest of it, we hungered after his face
for signs. And still
there was no news. The tall black hat tilted in interrogation
amid the hushed, suspended narrative,
and in answer they led him forth to the house
where the occupants were beginning to imagine
time in the permanent shape of a question,
that it might be the only bearable thing,
not this man with the darkly silver approach
of an angel, gravelly steps at midnight
at their dooryard

6

The sea is showing me how
to be one of its animals. I close my eyes
to it and still know my position
from the snug pressure of the waves,
by the place of sunlight on my cheeks,
by the shift into warmer or colder water.

And I know shallowness by listening—eyes
squeezed shut against the salt—listening to the way
rocks will suddenly split the ringing
with their own language like static
between the long music, the one note
of the deep.

7

They found some floats, a crate, some signs
of someone's passage, but finally, when recovered,
these things were only images
that served to bring the lost back home
for an hour, to carry them across the hollow
parentheses of no story at all—
the floats were the wrong color, that's all.

I don't know how to deny our relation,
the lost boat's and mine. If three
men vanish as only the closed sums of their own flesh,
if no one watches for a single pair of white arms
flashing in a slow approach and retreat from land
offshore, a tiny island named Lazarus, itself a metaphor
named to give hope to its one-time band of lepers
who thought they might rise out of their wasted skins
into a sudden body of redemption, just as
the christener of the *Archangel Michael* must have
imagined the danger of looking full into that light—

if none of this stands for the other,
then, reader—

8

Then, reader, a plane etching ever larger
circles on a map pinned to a cafe wall,

in a sky as empty as it was wide,
the circles broadening everywhere at once,

this plane found a boat adrift
off Egyptian shores

and what the sister knew as she ran fast
into the street

and what the mother knew as she rose
from her bed, and the father

as he hung up the radio phone
at the port police

and all that the crowd knew as it rushed
to news in front of the cafe

is that hunger met hunger,
alive, in the open sea.

Two

HOMETOWN

The jetway is already familiar, more mine
than the airstrip I lifted off from; and the rental
car is still dewed from its automated hosing
like the fresh start I imagine I have. I don't need
maps here, and can't say why
I'm like one of these people driving beside me
on the freeway, native. I can't tell them where
I've been, just names and dates. But all of us begin
to approximate our old selves, newly. Maybe
it happens in the garden, crushing lemon verbena
between our fingers, or when the wind lifts the summer
heat from the backs of our necks as we walk
up the big hill in the neighborhood, in the old stride,
to look down at the silky ship canal.
Nothing is lost or disappears. Between then and
what we can repeat, simply for the sake of repeating,
the past gets taken up, our topic,
our gathered filmy wrap carried
for its diaphanous beauty,
its exquisite weightlessness.

MOONWALKING ANNIVERSARY

Years ago we prepared
for moonwalking. First we went
to buy our first big television,
the whole family, as it was then,
whole, four of us in the new Volkswagen,
four of us straining painfully after news
of assassinations, invasions, staring at the maps
and arrows on our old, ghosty television.
Like all girls in the fifth grade I wore
my stainless steel POW bracelet
even in the bathtub, even in the pool,
and Blue Lake, where I forgot
his imprisonment briefly as I stood
on my brother's sloping shoulders, being thrown
or jumping. I think it was a Sunday?
I'm not sure but it was a Sunday type
of heat and enforced leisure as we shopped
through appliance stores, all of them
banked with color TVs which we couldn't
afford, all those rich pink moving mouths.
Ours was Zenith, nineteen-inch, black-and-white
console, furniture for the living room.
What a way to name a room—as if living didn't
take place anywhere else, but we knew
what we meant by it—our brief, whole
family life, in the living room,
at our Zenith, the bad news
temporarily switched to the chalky
tones of NASA and the endless gravelly-
voiced preparations. Then the hours of black
drifting we couldn't track, the sweet
Valentine voices out of the dark: Neil Armstrong,

a dreamboat name, as I twisted,
probably, my stainless steel
bracelet which I didn't remove for a whole
year—but can't remember his name—the lost
one, the tortured one—twisted
the bracelet in an agony of readiness
and desire, and knowledge, maybe,
that in my life, a normal life, as
all of them are, were revolutions. I knew this
because the announcers on the Zenith
looked at me squarely, earnestly,
and told me this. Told me
that everything was as new as me
practically, that I had practically
invented the world just by being here
now, in the living room, with the family
before the family ended,
ten years old but already in love a dozen ways,
already full of something far too big
to contain. This was history
on the Zenith, this was revolution
as Apollo turned away from its miniature Earth,
this was a dreamboat tethered
with heartbreaking fineness to our living room
as we four sat amazedly together,
waiting for the moonwalk.

THE REGULARS

Like a haunting we could predict them
more or less
and though they were annoying
we were more annoyed when they didn't show
to sit smugly with their "usuals," content
that here, at least,
it was someone's job to know exactly
what they needed.
Linda, whose pigmentless hair and watery eyes
could only come out after dark, her four
Sweet 'n Lows, half-coffee-half-hot-water,
dark bread only, heels if we had them.
Richard's daily pastry with which
he would sweeten unemployment,
and Brian at his writer's table in the corner, his rent
for five hours one large soup, one cherry
strudel, with endless decaf to be poured
whenever he was one-quarter inch down.
This to make sure he never felt a sense of progress
as he scribbled always in the middle of
his novel of twenty years.
They all tipped like the Depression,
as if their daily visits only served
to make them feel more homeless
no matter what their actual roof.
This was years ago.
I could still serve them to perfection,
remembering every stubborn taste like a harried mother,
and though I don't miss them I could make them happy,
knowing their happiness consisted of
not changing, ever.
All except one, the near-regular

whose name we never learned,
the young man who came once or twice a week
with his index cards
on which he had laboriously printed
everything he had done every day
since beginning rehabilitation from the accident.
He asked us what was good, took it
however it came, let it and his coffee cool
as he studied those cards, trying to see something
from the day before that might have happened to him.
A sweet guy and a good tipper.
Not a regular. He, nameless,
and without a pattern to follow,
who would give anything—thirty, forty percent—
to give up the chalky blackboards
on which could only be inscribed
what the single, solitary day had to offer.

TELEVISION MOVIE

In the first five minutes of the television movie
I recognize that what I see is already
the past, the nostalgic whole moment of carrying
out the supper casserole
before she loses him, has to
raise the kids, fight the bank, save the farm. It's there
in the restless panning camera and eerie absence
of background music. I want to tell the foolishly calm
fiction wife to know it—time like an uncracked
egg—take one good look out of harm's way
before memory steps in, gives her a perpetually
waltzing bridegroom who will from this moment forward
be unimpeachable; and before she gets stuck forever
with that musical score rushing in
to prove its argument that what is perfect
will leave us, is gone.

FATHER'S DAY

The day feels difficult, vagrant,
hot from the start, even in the park at 10 a.m. when I come holding
my paper cup of coffee. No one would say the day
wasn't beautiful; no one would say it wasn't drenched in green
underwater light.

One father, mine, sits far away and waits to die, mumbling
old grudges to his tireless self. After
the attendants have given up on his eyeglasses,
dentures, and shave, after he has batted
them all away in a rage, he sits

pissed off and bony, a gray silt of whiskers
and wild brows and flaking skin. He wanted to hit
his only granddaughter, brought blinking to him in flannel
at three months. But let us not dwell
on that. Let us dwell on the rhythmic ringing notes

of his hammer in the backyard thirty years ago,
when my father frowned in concentration
over the framing of a small house soon to be
shingled and roofed and painted the exact same shade
as the house we lived in in real life.

The small house was my brother's first house
of his own. I was a baby in a bonnet.
My brother and father conferred in serious tones
over the placement of the door. And everything was green:
the big house, the little house, the backyard and our tightly
     furled lives.

HANDSOME

For Carl E. Matson, 1905-1990

Oh he was, this stranger whose snapshot
I carry like a private investigator
matching faces in the crowd—the dark glossy
man beside my startlingly fawnlike mother
in 1947. They know something together,
something sexual and calmly resigned,
in their sunglasses and white bathing suits.

Then there are his arms folded across the workshirted
chest, the grin, the squarely faced front view
in full sun. No moods, ever, no posing, just an even
friendliness that left you with the impression,
mistaken, that he was tall. He could lead a woman across
the dance floor with such certain grace—
with never a lesson for it in his life—
that they hired him to teach it.
But you can't teach it, what you're born knowing,
what you walked around with, your one beautiful life,
and lay down with.

PETTY CRIME

She rose to a morning green and fragile
as a new twig. She kissed everyone

and for once didn't complain about herself,
her frailty, how it was good that we ate so well

because she couldn't take a thing in. She loved
that particular day—the flowering cherry and lilac.

She put her shoes in her empty handbag for the repairman.
She went down the apartment stairs, the difficult

porch steps, the rough walk. She made her way,
thin comma in the large text of the neighborhood,

and told her son later, that when the two kids
sped by and knocked her down in the bid

for her bag, her two pairs of run-down heels,
and as she fell forward listening

to bone go with the casual snap of pasta entering the cauldron,
she laughed; all she could do was laugh at what they were getting.

DRIVING MANHATTAN

This cabby plays with us—with me the fare
and baggage swaying in the back, and with this
river of moderate traffic on upper Fifth Avenue
along the sunny side of the new-leafed park. He guns it
and swerves, brakes, dips improbably back
into the moving lane. Clicks his tongue, riffs his horn, guns it
and weaves so breathtakingly fast that a second's miscalculation
would bring half a dozen paths to a crashing halt, forcing
us all to get out and exchange names—but we don't.
We stay in the fastest eddy
of midtown traffic, and just when we are seemingly
clogged once and for all in the gelatinous garment district
he plays soft staccato on the horn and speaks in his African
     language
to the cabby grinning in the next lane
who lets us in. *My cousin*, he says, and I picture cousinship
stepping in at all his stalled moments, looping him uptown,
downtown, the full deck of Jacks up his sleeve.

CENTRALIA STOP

The woman on the platform at Centralia holds an armful
of asters and intends to either meet the train
or see it off. She does not wave.
Her mouth opens, closes, as if air, great lungfuls,
were not her element, and she is drowning.
She has come with zinnias
and shouts something at the train
which does not stop.

Now she is small as a playing card in 52 passenger windows—
a bee crossed and inverted and converted to traveling impulse
along a chain of optic nerves.
Small and infinitely dividable woman
you were never matter to me.
You were a white moth in the corner of my eye
or a garden weed springing.
And now you are a story: someone's faded aunt on a porch swing
in Little Rock, someone's down-and-out wife
in Soda Springs. You may have been Class Valedictorian
and measured careful sentences at Commencement.
Huge woman with chrysanthemum
you lasted less than a second
and dissolved like a prairie.
Into your life—already crowded
with pruning scratches, a pinned seam, a permanent wave—
rush dahlias, and tomorrow, and tomorrow's train.

NORTH END, BOSTON

Nobody sitting in the shady square wants more
than this—the boy bouncing his tennis ball against
the mounted statue of Paul Revere. The boy is
fat, and not very good with his ball, but has a handsome
Italian face, and the beginning of a certain learned set
to the mouth: half-scowl and half-pleasure-kept-to-himself,
a man's guarded face. He gives us
our focus, this supremely secure, awkward boy
who has eaten biscotti in his mother's kitchen more
than he's pitched balls, so today his catcher's mitt
and green fuzzy ball and riding-up shorts seem like
a good sign, a possibility of everything returning
to ideal proportions, growing as scaled to nobility
as the rippling horse and tensely lithe rider who together
look only forward, into the abstract and heroic day.

FLAGSTAFF

I know he's in trouble, I heard him
telling someone on the pay phone
about no money, and late buses, and six hours
in the Flagstaff station. His wife's eyes are glazed
and she is silent. They are a handsome couple, they have
pretty babies. But the girl, who walks, and wants to,
can't get far. Her father swats her, whacks
her, making her cry. He holds his big brown hand flat
in front of her face so she can see how big, how
near, how ready to strike. Shut up, he says.
She tries to, but the hunger and fatigue
and sheer injustice work at her small lungs, filling
them until what she must do is explode
in a wail. He swings her up and storms out the door.
When they return she puffs her little breath
so as not to let any more grief build up all at once.
Covered by his jacket
in the plastic molded chair, bottle hanging
at her mouth, the girl keeps her eyes on some safe
middle distance. She is thinking her own thoughts, which lead
her to erupt in a cheerful babble of half song, half speech.
Shut up, her father says, lowering his face to hers.
No, she says, *no*. The father grins.
The mother suddenly puts down the newborn and hefts
the girl up and off into the women's restroom. There she will say
don't make your daddy mad, because she knows.
She thought she had all the power once when she leaned
before a restroom mirror just like this one and re-reddened
her mouth like a clenched rose before
they went for a drive. She wore thin
little heels then, that clicked on a cold brick floor like
this one. He always said back then that one look from her

could strike him down. Don't make your daddy mad
she will say, running the warm water to play in, starting
all the automatic dryers in a row. The little girl carries
her laugh all the way back out to the lobby, where her daddy
slumps beside her baby brother. Her father has less
than a dollar in his pocket like a baby, like a fool.
Shut up, her mother says, before the father can,
and the girl does. Don't think that when he frowns down
at her and puts out his hand, not unkindly,
what shines out of her eyes isn't pure light.
She has a mouth shaped like a little rose
and when he swoops her up and grins, the rose opens
to chortle because she adores him,
fears him, adores him.

THE BOYFRIEND

Her daddy can still see her driving
his golf cart, long blonde hair
permed into kinky waves because she was
artistic that way. Who knows—maybe she would have
been a hairdresser, with her flair.
"She was an up type of girl,"
her daddy said, people saw
her at the club, always laughing, "What a doll,"
they told him. "From her father's standpoint,
she was perfect."

"It sucks being you Amy" her boyfriend said
as he shoved the body into the pond.
Her head was in a plastic bag, bubbles streamed up
to the surface like silver confetti as the cinder blocks
pulled her down.
But she was dead before she hit the water.
She was dead as soon as she went into the woods
with Jamie, her boyfriend, the guy
who loved her, who ran his fingers
through those permed waves—just as Amy
ran hers through her cut paper pom-poms, taking out
the tangles after a game. Amy was 14,
she flirted. But then she went into the woods with Jamie
("Jamie, it always seemed to be more serious
to him. It wouldn't stop with a slap to the mouth")
went into the woods
to be accused, to argue,
to kiss and make up but instead ("He doesn't know
his own strength") Jamie showed her the knife,
made sure she saw it go in, watched her eyes
as she watched the first few plunges.

It sucks being you Amy. You did it all the way
you were supposed to: you cheered and leaped into the air
for them, you never stopped smiling and laughing
for them, you worked hard on your hair, you had
a serious boyfriend.
You did everything right.
You were perfect, doll.

ALMOST TO SOCIAL HILL

It began in Memphis, the rowdy boys
with their 7-card stud in the back of the bus,
their cries of outrage as they all lost one by one.
In Little Rock it got worse. Passengers pursed
their lips when the band of them reboarded single-file
doing a rap song and a slow-lorus robot dance, until
the old white lady in the front seat of all people
broke the ice, drawled, *Y'all take
a Geritol tablet?* And the leader in his black
and gold metallic sweats bowed to her with extreme
courtesy and said *Yes ma'am, I did take
a Geritol tablet.* But it was louder and drunker
after that, and when the bus driver pulled over
to warn them they started a guerilla campaign
against the driver, rolling empty bottles up the dark
aisle, muttering *motherfucker* in the back. At Hot Springs,
Arkansas, with a big new Hilton rising improbably
out of the bare hills, we stopped for a stretch and to unload
freight—thousands and thousands of crickets
shipped in for bait, singing from their boxes on the dolly
in concentrated form, like dusk-in-a-can
or a fishing lake on CD. It was calm there, with our crickets,
and the two teenage sisters who strolled to meet
the bus—not anyone in particular, but just the bus
itself, the event of us. They were busting out
with kids—one pregnant and one hauling a toddler—
and joking around, laughing
in the heat as it got dark.
We got rolling again, and the boys started up
again, and then they had to go. The driver parked
and got out at the gas station to make his call and Mr.
Black-and-Gold got out long enough to make a careful

pyramid of his empties in front of the unleaded pump.
Unleaded, he explained. That was a big part of the effect.
The police came from behind. They invited him
to go with them. When the black boys were spread-eagled
against the squad car being frisked by the white cops
and the black driver stood by with their tickets in his hand,
and the black and white passengers looked on, we felt
fear. That this moment would suddenly rise up
and be about something huge and untenable, that the crickets
we left down the road would not be enough, or the soft red
glow of the Hilton with its miraculous waters would not be
enough to offset it. Then the driver slid
the door shut behind him with that mechanical sigh sound,
and it sounded just like it was supposed to when the bus
was just about to change gears and start going somewhere.
One by one the little overhead lights blinked off like reverse
stars. The driver settled into his headphones. My own
announced that I could go somewhere and sign
the Put-Elvis-On-A-Stamp petition
and then a song came on from Brian to the girl
he was going to marry the next day. I kept waiting for
words to the song, but it was just music. Their last date
before real life was right now and their song kept
playing wordlessly—no promises, no stories of looking back.
It is five miles to Social Hill, Arkansas, and eight miles
beyond that will be Friendship, the direction from which those
truckers are coming in a long convoy, their lights strung
evenly together in the night.

THREE

FLORIDA

My skin remembers this the way a dream
remembers a place you've never been—in soft swatches
of familiarity that won't be stitched together
into what you can be sure of.

I'm early, so I wait curbside at the airport,
blinking in the unexpected
light as the bus traffic loops in and out
to meet us. People are always leaving

and returning; every second someone kisses
someone else and steps into the large
rings of transit. But so far I am alone, so I concentrate
on my presence in this unseasonable light,

my matter-of-fact delivery into it, and the obscure
good fortune of these palms. They rustle dryly,
as beautifully thin and full of sad secrets
as film stars. I wonder how it is I can know you so instantly

behind your sunglasses, in a rental car, at 50 yards,
as though your features were my new paradigm
for touching ground. Now you loop over to where I stand
and this light is brilliant and warm, and not more
than I can take in.

WAITING FOR YOU

Waiting for you I am alert
padding around the room, checking
the mirror again, as if it were her
I waited for, the rose-lit girl in the antique
glass, old scratches diffusing the angle
of her gaze so that as she composes
herself, practicing her mouths, I feel
admiration for her softness because within
I tighten; I feel unbidden; I wait.
I can call her forth at my desire. She waits
for me, slides central in the frame, looks
expectant. Behind the wall next door
a man I don't know is in for the evening.
His TV is an inarticulate whisper. Above it all
he clears his throat, in the neighbor language
we have—assertions of our presence against
silence, against surfaces, knowing another to eavesdrop.
And any second now you will split time with your ring,
your ring making me forget time, and in forgetting
time forget reflection, so that one of us
will leave the room, shutting lights and doors,
coming to meet you.

IT WAS WHEN

Poised there, on the brink of calling
myself a year older, somewhere after
midnight, legally older, but
before the actual hour—and certainly before
the hour in pale blue Pacific time when
my mother woke to broken water—
in that cradle of not knowing my age,

that darkness, I heard it storm outside
I heard myself not sleep
I heard sirens rush to danger
I heard you sleep
and the wind that pressed itself through
the window seams came like someone's cold hand
saying rest from these hot bodies,
trust me, trust me.

The next day was about to start itself from scratch
and I had no reason not to
so I lay still, neither one age nor the other
neither with you nor without you
too hot and too cold I lay there hoping.

THE WATERS AT LISDOONVARNA

In the town where maids are matched
to farming lads, we split ourselves
along our one new seam
and divided left and right into the spa.
My country-bred attendant all in white
wrapped me in thick terry, fussed
with the temperature of my sulphur-
yellow bath, until she was content.
She eased me in as if I faced great
peril there. Nothing to do but float
pale and loose of joint within
the steaming hollow porcelain

as somewhere you floated too, your man
softly treading in and out to touch
the water, open valves and shut, leave
you to your thoughts. This privacy
was strange—my flesh still raw and bearing marks
of you. We were to be our own one sex here,
single and restored, to each absorb
the properties of oldest stone dissolved
within the aquifer, and no one knew
by what exchange of molecules we would
arise from this immersion changed,
as flushed and shiny as two newborns,
searching for each other.

FARM ANIMALS

My husband stalks them, the visiting
American cousin photographing farm animals.
He touches one whenever they let him: the hot breath
of a donkey; the drool of cattle; the skittish, irritated
shufflings of the new mothers we find everywhere
this June.

There is a hill that his grandfather walked to,
and, as he told it, took one last look back at his cottage
before walking down the other side in thick boots,
down to the road, which led to the harbor.

It took five hours to fly back to Ireland, for a young man
and his wife of one day, back to the hill in Kilshanney,
where this groom, this grandson, would like most to help this new-
born calf to its feet. The calf wants most
to kneel in the gloom of the shed on hay and suck
my husband's finger. My husband tries tenderly to coax
it to its feet, on pipe-stem legs, the way it must start.

WIFERY

After the gentle click of the latch behind him
the house readjusts to a new order,
its details trembling on a string of lists:
walk to market, walk to cleaners, start stew.
She is testing a life as readymade for her
as love, how the shape of someone's
shoulders suddenly come to mean *this much*;
this far and no farther. With utter
certainty she crushes the iced slush underfoot
in a morning as wide-open and delicate as
the mouth of a teacup: she must have
12 small white onions, she must have
bleeding cubes of stewing beef, and cream
of tartar for biscuits. The summer night they met
she said, I can't cook, I don't cook.
Now in winter the blade makes neat work
of her lie, quartering potatoes
glistening in their nudity, filling the simmering
pot to its fragrant hissing lip.

HOUSEHUNTING AFTER A QUARREL

22 Ash Street is cold but we are not to mind
our realtor says, thumping silent radiators
as she leads us in. The chandelier hangs low
over the ghost of a dining table, incandescent
with crystal and candlelight. Cabbage roses
climb the walls, brightening in the squares of missing
pictures. Upstairs the rooms are pastel-papered for baby,
broncos for a little buckaroo, bouquets for Mother and Father,
and pale pink for a musty guest. The realtor demonstrates
the connecting nature of the house, doors you can open
like a string of pearls between the rooms, or a suite
of slamming that could carry you as far as anger.
We drive after her to Lakeside Way,
where a pair of owners has refused to return
from Florida. They will make us a gift
of chenille-tufted beds, rush-caned rockers, a phonograph rack,
a garden hose. The house is faintly medicinal
and they want us to have it all—the morning cup of Sanka
facing the lake, wheat toast from the burnt orange breadbox,
crocheted webs draping the sofa.
By the time we have searched with a flashlight
through the day's last crumbling Victorian, echoing empty
except for the Yellowstone and Newport pennants,
we are sick of all their lives, the small bits of their board games
sticking to our shoes. The realtor totters and freezes in her heels
under the enlarged November moon, precarious
on the flagstone steps we could buy and insure,
ankle deep in the brittle leaves that might be ours to sweep away.
She claps her little bunches of keys to keep warm and promises
to find it, whatever street it's on,
something that we can pay for, something we can fix,
and swears that we'll be happy there.

WORRY

When worry moved in it clasped itself
like a boss's large hand amicable at the back
of the neck, one finger pointing to the base
of the skull, the others splayed toward the slope
the shoulder makes. With worry hooked
there so that the head not quite rested against it,
the head was suddenly aware of its own weight,
like a bloom on a too-thin stem,
wagging askew of the plumb line that falls from crown
to footsole. Then walking became
walking with the head,
holding it as you hold a part-time job,
that extra obligation, that due you pay
to the guiding avuncular palm facing you
toward your future.

STUBBORNNESS

The day is bright and zero,
full of shocks everywhere I touch;
I am wrapped,
swaddled, sunglassed,
my head is down.
From somewhere a white
inarticulate call. My husband,
anonymous in wool, across
the street. We have startled
each other. We both raise
a gloved hand. We could not
hear if we tried speech.
Going in opposite directions
we do not think it worthwhile
to cross the street. If I said
I'm sorry now, he would not
hear it. If he said
I love you I could only
shake my head
and pantomime a shrug.

FIELD TRIP

Quabbin Reservoir, Massachusetts

We had planned to be the only ones
to venture the frozen wind,
to follow snowtracks we could not read
and argue meanings with the convictions
of autodidacts: *long hind foot
of rabbit startled into brush-leap.*

In fact we joined a knot of watchers
already huddled on the shore
with equipment more determined
than ours—field glasses with super-zoom,
telescopes, tripods.

If the eagles came for them,
what would it mean? That those waiting
had withstood inhuman gusts
as offering, to be in brief one-way
contact. I too find myself
hoping for the gift appearance,
eagles coasting on the invisible slopes
of our leaning toward them, then their positive
return to aerie where a mate
will recognize only one other, both
of them bound by the same law
to gather and shield,
gather and shield,
against this opening field of winter wind,
this dazzling brightness of nothing.

MRS. CHILD ON THE DANGERS OF TRAVEL

To make a long story short,
the farmer and his wife conclude to go to Quebec,
just to show they had a *right*
to put themselves to inconvenience, if they pleased.

> *The last ice was cracking on the pond,*
> *and the blue overhead seemed to promise*
> *limitless future, and for once the stores*
> *had lasted through the winter, and all of us*
> *were sound. Then as I packed the heavier wools*
> *in camphor and tobacco leaves, and polished*
> *the andirons to wrap in papers, and dragged*
> *the rugs outside to air, I saw an image:*
> *two of us again, trim and eager,*
> *leaning at the rail of a white boat.*

They went; spent all their money;
had a watch stolen from them in the steamboat;
were dreadfully seasick off Point Judith;
came home tired, and dusty.

> *We were nervous with excitement getting on,*
> *managing our small suitcases and lunchbox,*
> *and so when the sudden windstorm hit,*
> *darkening the waves and sky to lead,*
> *we found ourselves held by that metallic*
> *wind and gripping one another by the*
> *wrists, as if we were each other's last proof*
> *of land. I had almost forgotten how it felt*
> *to lean into his rescue; or what his face*
> *at nineteen was like, scared and stubborn.*

And what do you get in return
for all this? Some pleasant scenes,
which will soon seem to you like a dream;
some pleasant faces, which you will never see again.

It's true the babe was sick on our return,
the girl had kept her too long in a draft.
The loss of Jacob's father's watch comes hard,
and we will have to make economies
this spring. Our little house feels extra
snug right now, the cooking fire bright
and burning low. And simple porridge seems
a feast, because we eat it at our own
pine board. I almost think we hadn't been
away—but then I see us, different in
our traveling suits, among the strangers roaming
on the decks. I see us as they might have done:
not the tired farmer and his wife
but that tall man there, his arm behind the dame
to steady her. They look like neat and decent
folk, youthful still, and strong. And if
frequent trusting glance be any guide,
some happiness, I think, between them.

THE CROSSING

We weren't homesick exactly,
what was to regret, the dark stone cottage
the thin square of soil. Although we
missed the sauna, certainly—
I was born in it, and Celia, and Warner.
Those nights that took up most of the day in winter,
with no letter from Father, we heated the stones
until you could see through them
to the fire inside; that warmed us.
We huddled together, sweating; the tang of the birch leaves
floated in steam as we scrubbed each other's backs.

Then the letter, with Father's stabbings
on thin American paper telling us to come.
With Mother in her ninth month I took
charge of the packing
because she wouldn't be postponed.
But we didn't have so much to keep us, after all:
a packet of photos, some clothes, the wedding tablecloth.

No, we weren't homesick, but sick for want
of home, longing through the queasy swells and pitches
for the land that Father promised—
bright, sunny, and almost free
for taking. Walter was born on the crossing.
A funny, no citizen birth.
I helped but he came easy, maybe because of the rocking,
and Mother lay back in her bunk
while I herded the little ones to the galley door
for scraps. Warm greasy gusts
came swinging out with each crewhand on an errand.
They let us peel potatoes for extra milk.

In Michigan it snows like Lehtimaki. Father built a sauna.
He goes to the mines each morning before light
and for me and Mother it is just about the same.
We do the washing, bake, feed the children. The company
house is bigger than our stone cottage was
but not as strong, so storms get in, and we are
always busy stopping drafts.
Saturday night is for sauna. Father and our uncles first,
then Mother and we children. It is like being rich,
the sauna, like choosing exactly
where you would be if you could.

The spring baby will be our first
American, the first to have the new name
right from birth. Mother practices writing it
for the certificate. She goes out of her way
to avoid bad omens, but I don't believe in them.
I know this is a lucky country.
I can see already the power
of the new name, which we trace
again and again from the block letter language
of our landing papers.

NEAR RELATION

On a country lane in Lancaster
we are the ones who pull over to the side,
trying to glimpse the faces sealed
within the buggy pulled toylike
behind the robust clopping chestnut.
It was a gift to come upon
the Amish in such converging numbers
as they walked straightbacked in families
to Sunday suppers, seeing them raise
their hands in friendly salute
even to the gaping strangers, us.

I am ashamed to want their photo
so badly—embarrassed to call them scenic
when they are so perfectly being themselves.
I compromise, allowing distance
to claim them. Now they are anonymous
figures merging black-cloaked
with the horizon, lost to me.

On our way back to Philadelphia
the turnpike is torn up with repairs.
Signs blinking every half-mile warn
of no shoulder, narrow lanes, sudden changes.
The trick is to keep your car speeding ahead
as if the road bore you no ill will.
Presidential candidates argue
over the radio in our darkened car.
The incumbent tells us in a pleased tone
that we have never been more secure;
the challenger is hoarse with repeated warnings.

The Amish children, now asleep,
looked back at us with interest.
What are they told of the world
and its hazards? How many will ever
be tourist among us? The road is being
improved, says the sign, so it
is temporarily unsafe.
And now we are running out of gas
and the only exit takes us to
this neighborhood which we think
is a ghetto. The candidates murmur
their plans to improve ghettos.

We are lost in this dark where we imagine that
no one will help us, and we have begun to argue
about who led us here, settling the matter
with silence.
The cop and the kid on the corner point in unison
to the gas station which was always
just around the corner.

My mother's father was a Mennonite,
raised to kneel three times a day.
I came among the Amish to sightsee
at his birthplace and my secret
wish was that I could have somehow
owned the knowledge of his faith,
that it might discover me to be
a near relation coming home,
both prodigal and saved.

DURABLE GOODS

As if we were responding to
the clarion call of rising
consumer confidence
we followed the salesman,
our pied piper, through
all the rooms of his make-believe
house—the drift from empire
to federal and over to mission,
the casual plush arrangements
designed to seduce us into thinking
we could call this home.
Samplers in the bears' cottage
we tried on rockers, recliners
wings, clubs, looking to be
taken in. *Too big*,
the salesman scolded
as I stretched to touch the floor,
too small, he frowned
as my husband folded himself up.
Just right, he beamed,
as we took turns fitting
perfectly, and he scratched
our order on the pad
in secret hieroglyphs.

Waiting for our new chair
means sitting on the old furniture
we bought separately, before we
could imagine the dog with spots,
the children each with a name
stored in keeping like holiday lace.
We're all impatient for the new chair,

the whole imaginary family
swirling around the living room
waiting to shuck off the makeshift,
waiting with the foolish glee
of householders
for permanent things.

At night you sometimes touch my face
as if its contours in the dark
could tell you
what you need to know. Beyond
the nearness of lips, cheeks, closed eyes
what you need to know is this:
you are my rising certainty,
you are the beginning of this story,
you are my durable good.

"The Boyfriend" (35): The poem is dedicated to Amy Carnevale, who was murdered by her boyfriend at the age of fourteen on August 23, 1991. All quotations are from articles in *The Boston Globe* and *The Boston Herald* appearing August 29, 1991, the day after Amy's body was pulled from Shoe Pond in Beverly, Massachusetts.

"Mrs. Child on the Dangers of Travel" (51): Mrs. Child's voice in the poem is quoted from her book *The American Frugal Housewife*, originally published in Boston in 1832 by Carter, Hendee, and Co.; reprinted in a facsimile edition by Applewood Books of Boston and Cambridge.

RECENT TITLES FROM ALICE JAMES BOOKS

To the Left of the Worshiper Jeffrey Greene

The Knot Alice Jones

The Secretary Parables Nancy Lagomarsino

Vox Angelica Timothy Liu

This Particular Earthly Scene Margaret Lloyd

Sea Level Suzanne Matson

Home Country Cheryl Savageau

Infrequent Mysteries Pamela Stewart

The River at Wolf Jean Valentine

Traveling Mercies David Williams

Alice James Books has been publishing poetry since 1973. One of the few presses in the country that is run collectively, the cooperative selects manuscripts for publication and the new authors become active members of the press, participating in editorial and production activities. The press was named for Alice James, sister of William and Henry, whose gift for writing was ignored and whose fine journal did not appear in print until after her death.